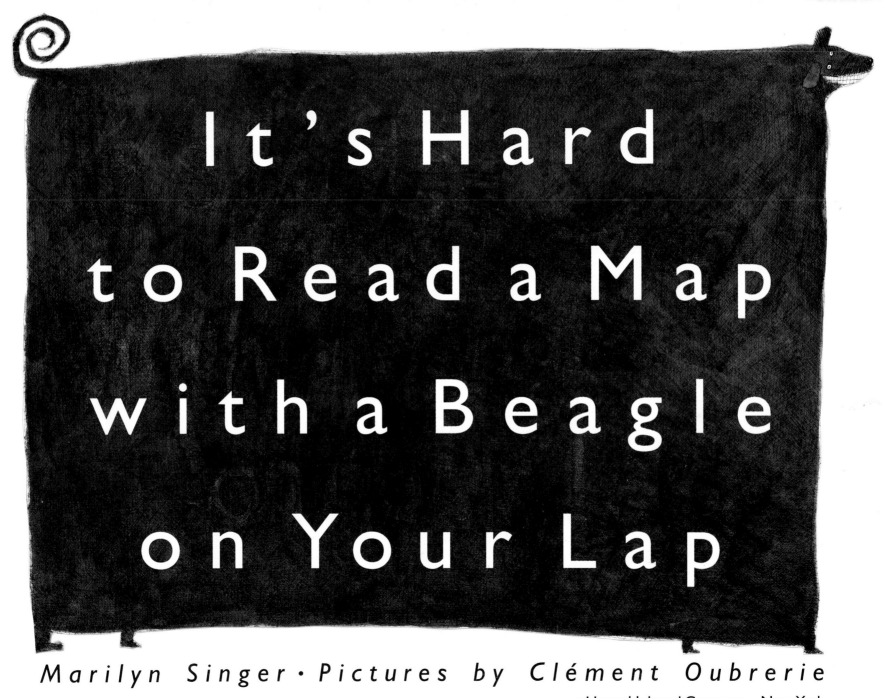

It's Hard to Read a Map with a Beagle on Your Lap

Marilyn Singer · Pictures by Clément Oubrerie

Henry Holt and Company · New York

To Jay and Oak Kerig
　　　　　　—M. S.

To my cat

　　　　　　—C. O.

Acknowledgments

Thanks to Steve Aronson, Nola Thacker, Karen Wojtyla,
Brenda Bowen, Simone Kaplan, and Maryann Leffingwell.
　　　　　　—M. S.

Text copyright © 1993 by Marilyn Singer
Illustrations copyright © 1993 by Clément Oubrerie
All rights reserved, including the right to reproduce
this book or portions thereof in any form.
First edition
Published by Henry Holt and Company, Inc., 115 West 18th Street,
New York, New York 10011.
Published simultaneously in Canada by Fitzhenry & Whiteside Ltd.,
91 Granton Drive, Richmond Hill, Ontario L4B 2N5.

Library of Congress Cataloging-in-Publication Data
Singer, Marilyn.
　　It's hard to read a map with a beagle on your lap / Marilyn Singer;
　　pictures by Clément Oubrerie.
　　Summary: A collection of playful poems about dogs.
　　ISBN 0-8050-2201-5 (alk. paper)
　　1. Dogs—Juvenile poetry.　2. Children's poetry, American.
　[1. Dogs—Poetry.　2. American poetry.]　I. Oubrerie, Clément, ill.
　PS3569.I546I8　1993　　811'.54—dc20　　　92-26166

Designed by Paula R. Szafranski

Printed in the United States of America on acid-free paper. ∞

10　9　8　7　6　5　4　3　2　1

It's hard to read a map
With a beagle on your lap

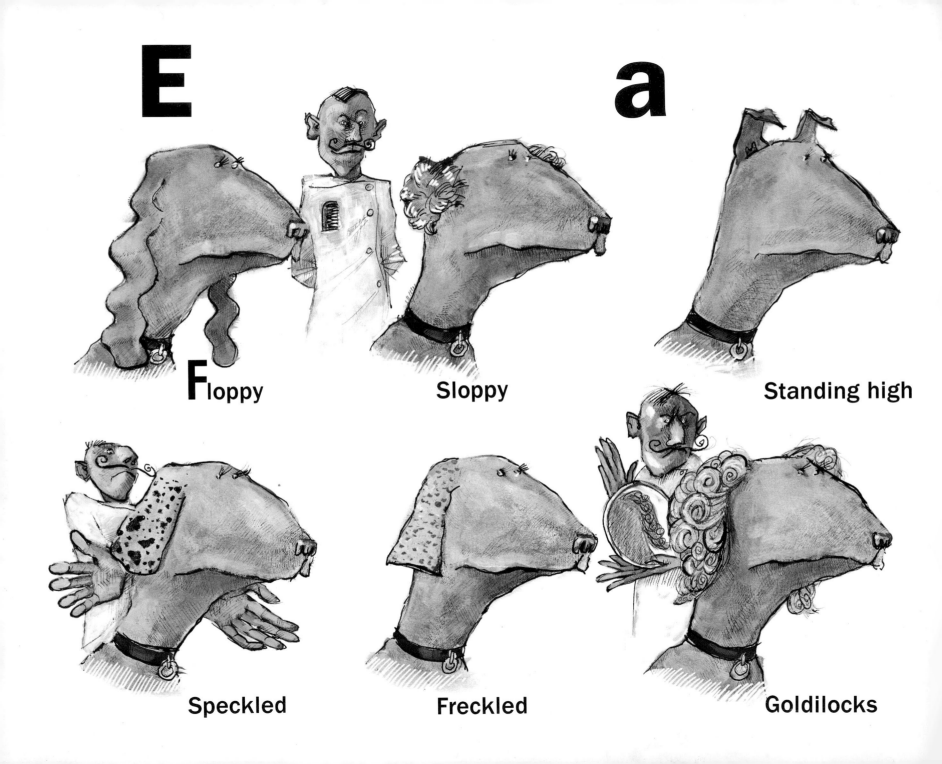

Floppy

Sloppy

Standing high

Speckled

Freckled

Goldilocks

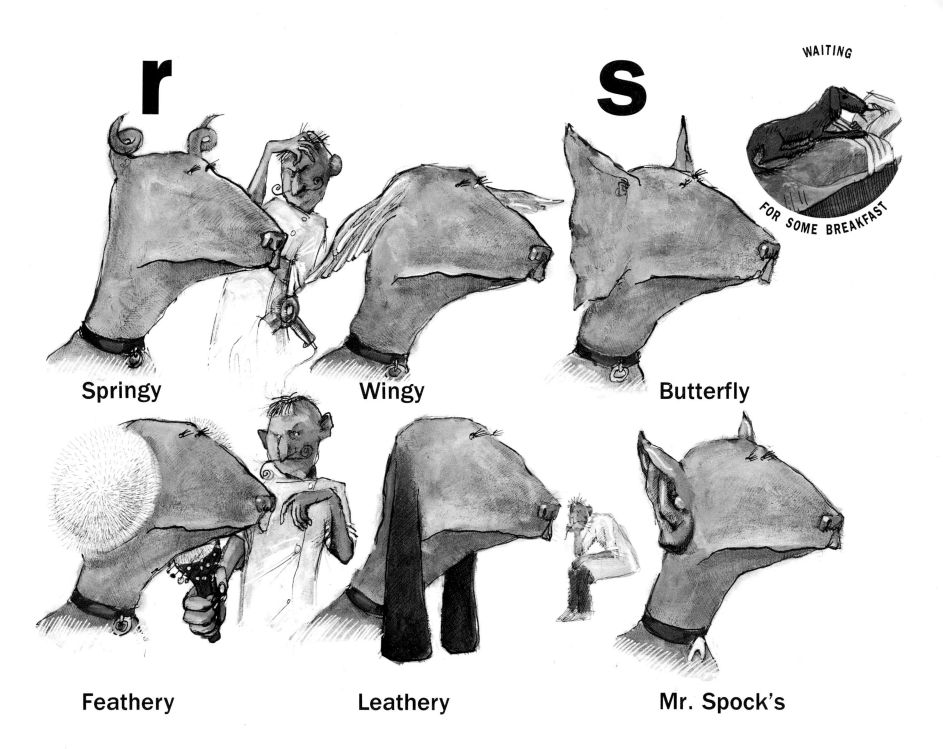

r

s

WAITING FOR SOME BREAKFAST

Springy

Wingy

Butterfly

Feathery

Leathery

Mr. Spock's

Nothing on a
bulldog's face
Seems to have a proper place
His eyelids droop
His jaws are square
His jowls are beyond compare
His nose looks like he's had a fight
He's got a great big underbite
You look at him and have to hoot
He's so ugly that
he's cute

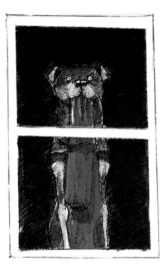

FOR A SNACK

When a rottweiler feels rotten
   Does he stuff his ears with cotton?
Does he sulk upon his bed
   A pile of pillows on his head?
Does he stomp around and shout
   "You guys had better let me out"?
Does he tear up someone's sweater?
   Or just wait till things get better?

There once was a young weimaraner
Who frequently ate in a diner
At the counter she'd sit
Where she made quite a hit
Though she thought that a booth would be finer

There once was a golden retriever At a ball game he got in a fever He brought back the bats the helmets and hats And then carried off the reliever

WAITING TO GO SOMEWHERE

A dachshund's body's very long

His legs are very short   It's obvious that basketball will never be his sport

He stinks at rinks and also links and at the tennis court

Dogs do not do the dishes
They do not push a broom
They do not weed the garden
They never clean their room
Dogs do not cook their dinner
Through homework they don't slog
You must agree
It's plain to see
No dog works like a dog

A Saint Bernard made my aunt faint
When he got into cans of paint
Galloped through her nice clean halls
Left his paw prints on her walls

She looked into his big brown eyes
And made this sad complaint
"I know that you're a Bernie
But you'll never be a saint."

WAITING
IN THE HALL

A Mexican hairless will not shed
Upon your sofa or your bed
You will not need to fetch a broom
Every time she leaves the room
Or take a vacuum to your clothes
Just because she'd sat on those
The time you save not cleaning hair
Will let you knit her underwear

Fur

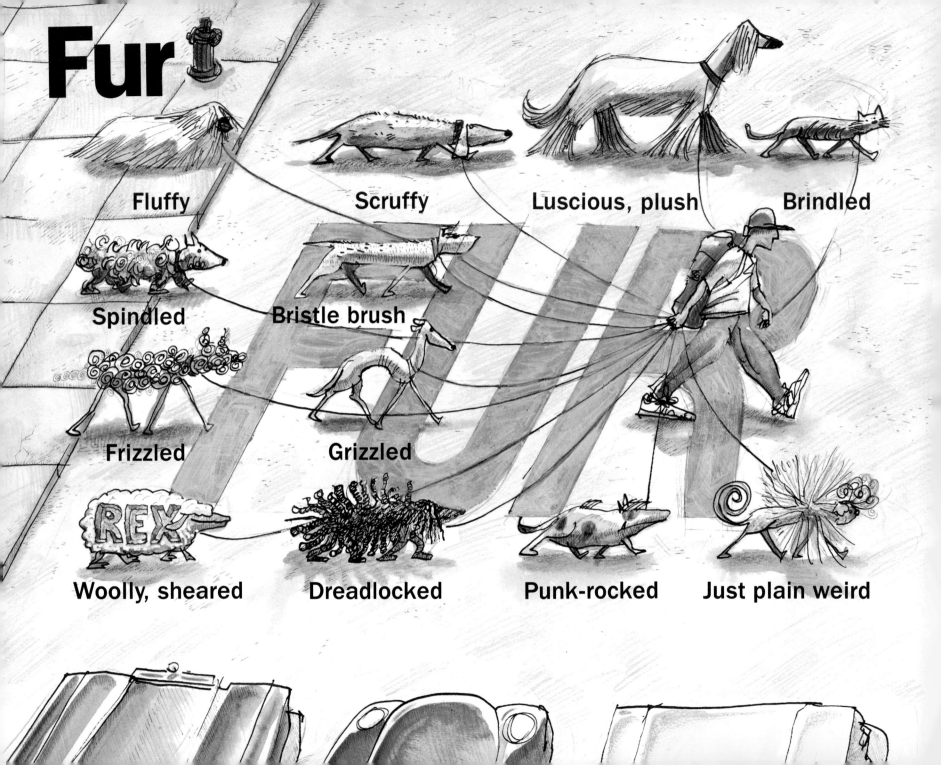

Fluffy

Scruffy

Luscious, plush

Brindled

Spindled

Bristle brush

Frizzled

Grizzled

Woolly, sheared

Dreadlocked

Punk-rocked

Just plain weird

WAITING

IN THE SPRINGTIME

Some canines sing soprano
Some pooches only bass
Some sit while they are singing
But others like to pace
Some sing when they hear sirens
Some when they have the blues
Mine vocalizes daily
To the seven A.M. news

Standing by a picket fence
A dalmatian caused confusion
I wondered if he was a dog
Or an optical illusion

I wouldn't want to tackle
An irritated jackal
I confess I'd care to mess
With a wolf pack even less
But I'd rather face their wrath
Than give my basset hound a bath

Dogs like to stop at hydrants
They like to stop at trees
They like to lean out windows
And catch a little breeze
They like to sleep on sofas
Instead of on the floor
They like to crawl in bed with you
And then they like to snore

Just because a schnauzer's drowsy
It's not nice to say he's lousy
It's not true that he's a loser
He's just what you'd call a schnoozer

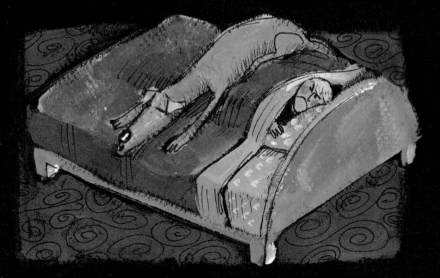

When a Belgian shepherd cannot sleep
Does she lie there counting sheep?
Could she number bears or leopards?
Or does she just count other shepherds?

At night I go to bed and dream
That I'm a movie star
I own a big white mansion
I drive a big red car
At night while I have visions
Of being someone classy
I wonder if my puppy dreams
She's Rin Tin Tin or Lassie

It's hard to waltz with grace

WAITING AT THE STORE

While a bloodhound licks your face

My German shepherd's very smart
At doing lots of tricks
She leaps right over fences
To fetch you back some sticks
She climbs up ladders
Jumps through hoops
And maybe even skis
But tell me why
With all those brains
She can't get rid of fleas

You can give him silken cushions
You can let him sleep real late
You can feed him tasty tidbits
off a shiny silver plate
You can try to entertain him
You can do your best to please
But nothing ever satisfies
a picky Pekingese

WAITING TO DISCOVER

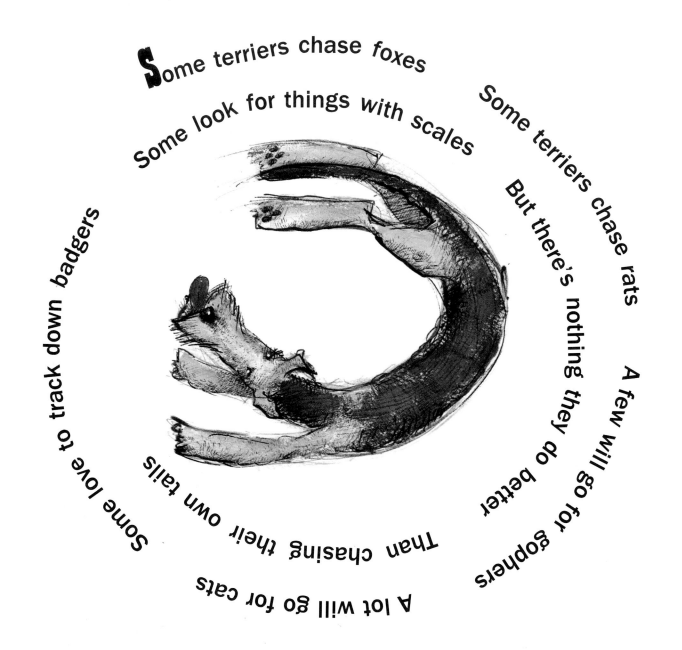

Some terriers chase foxes

Some look for things with scales

Some terriers chase rats

But there's nothing they do better

A few will go for gophers

Than chasing their own tails

A lot will go for cats

Some love to track down badgers

When a sheepdog's shorn
does he suffer scorn?
Do the lambs all laugh
'cause he looks like half
of the dog he was
when he had his fuzz?
Does he feel a fool?
Or does he just feel cool?

HE'LL HAVE TO WAIT
SOME MORE

A mongrel I know goes through streaks
Where she's crazy for whatever reeks
    She took a grand tour
    Through a field of manure—
We couldn't go near her for weeks

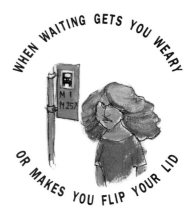

My puppy has a pointer's tail
Her body's like a spitz
She has an Irish wolfhound's head
Plus several other bits
Her ears look like a basset hound's
Except they're not as big
But when she stuffs her face with food
She's totally a pig

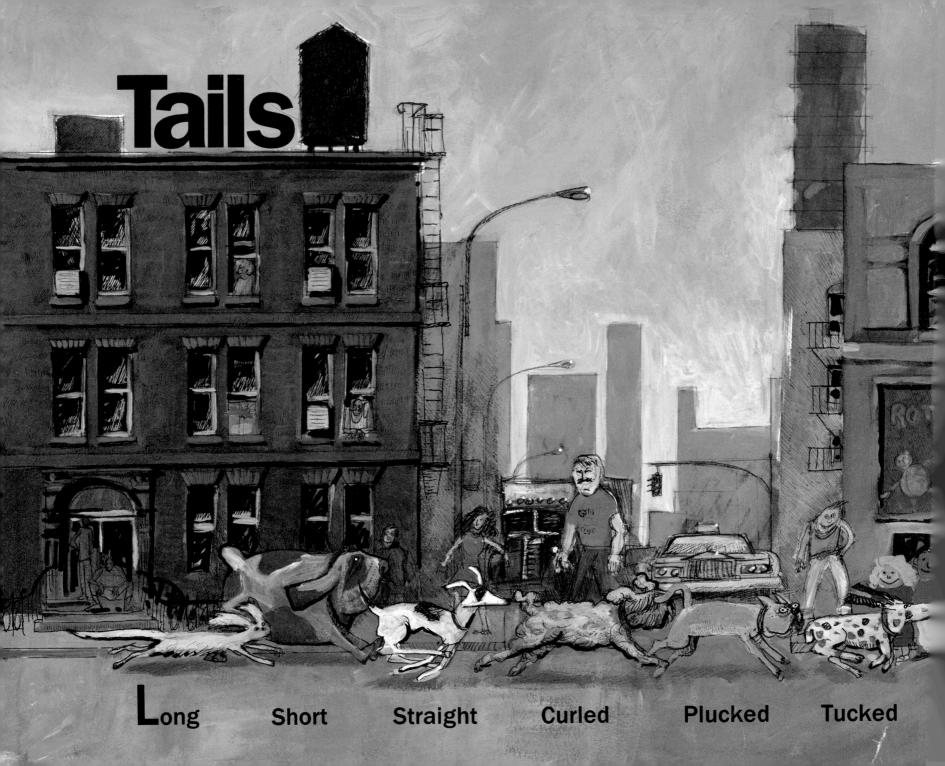

Tails

Long   Short   Straight   Curled   Plucked   Tucked

JUST THINK—A DOG CAN DO IT MUCH BETTER THAN A KID

Unfurled   Loopy   Droopy   Feather duster   Pom-pom   Tom-tom

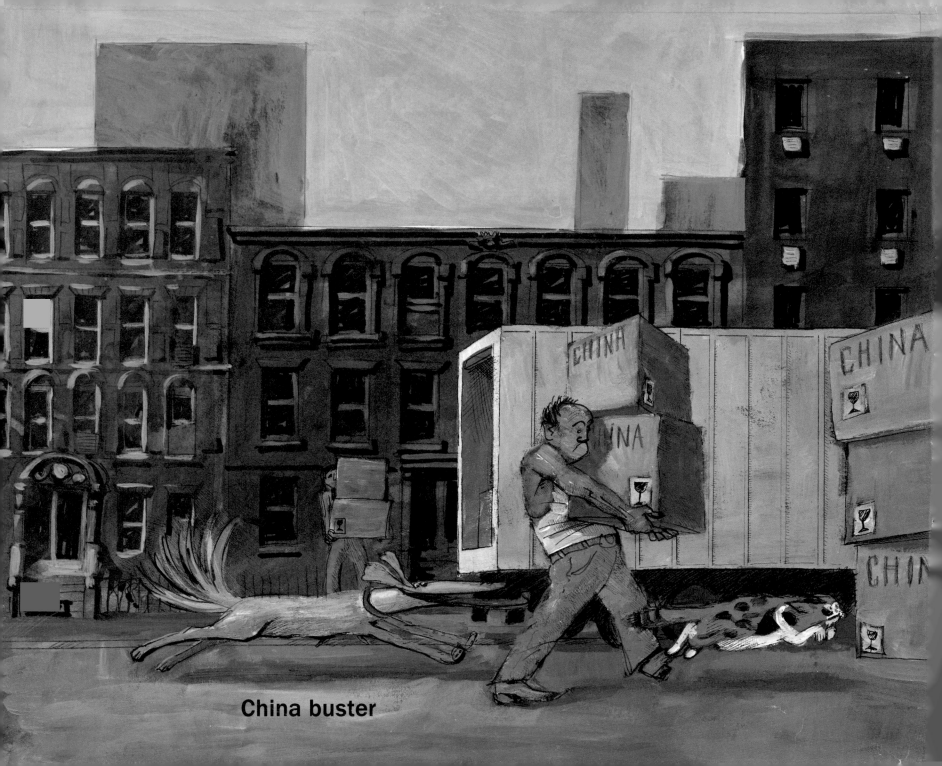

China buster